Study Guide

Justice, Crime & Ethics

fourth edition

Prepared by Wayne Gillespie
East Tennessee State University

anderson publishing co.
2035 Reading Road
Cincinnati, OH 45202
800-582-7295

Justice, Crime and Ethics, Fourth Edition
STUDY GUIDE

Copyright © 2002
Anderson Publishing Co.
2035 Reading Rd.
Cincinnati, OH 45202

Phone 800.582.7295 or 513.421.4142
Web Site www.andersonpublishing.com

This Study Guide was designed to be used in conjunction with
Justice, Crime and Ethics, 4th ed. © 2002 by Anderson Publishing Co. (ISBN: 1-58360-543-6)

EDITOR Ellen S. Boyne • ACQUISITIONS EDITOR Michael C. Braswell

Table of Contents

Chapter 1

Ethics, Crime, and Justice:
An Introductory Note to Students

by Michael C. Braswell

Key Concepts

ethics
morals
wholesight

Introduction

In a general sense, ethics is the study of right and wrong, good and evil. It is a creative endeavor in which a number of our beliefs and assumptions will be challenged. The study of ethics encompasses a variety of different disciplines that contribute to criminal justice, including law, economics, psychology, sociology, philosophy, and theology. For the purposes of this text, the terms "ethical" and "moral" will be used interchangeably.

Our beliefs and values regarding right and wrong are shaped by our parents and friends, by the communities of which we are a part, and by our own perceptions. The study of ethics involves all aspects of who we are—our minds, hearts, relationships with each other, and the intentions and motives for our actions regarding both our inner and outer environment. Being unethical is not simply committing an evil or wrongful act (commission), it is also a matter of being an indirect accomplice to evil by silently standing by when the evil occurs (omission). Unethical acts have to do with both commission and omission. The study of ethics involves a sense of community that includes our family, neighbors, and even the air we breathe.

Three Contexts for Understanding Justice, Crime, and Ethics

The first context is the *personal* one. When studying others we find ourselves questioning and testing our own personal sense of values and ethics. While our examination of the issues should be objective, it should also be personal.

Another broad context is the *social* one, through which we relate to others in our community, both directly and indirectly. Persons do not commit crimes in

1

isolation. Crimes require circumstances and victims. The social context suggests that we need to better understand the conditions and environments that encourage people to become criminals.

The third context is perhaps the most specific one and centers around the *criminal justice process*. A new law being proposed regarding the punishment of offenders needs to be explored in terms of personal beliefs and in terms of the social context of how it will affect the community.

The Five Goals for Exploring Ethics

The initial goal is to *become more aware and open to moral and ethical issues*. In doing this, we discover there is often a difference between appearances and reality—things are often not what they seem. The broad range of moral issues reminds us that where justice is concerned, our personal values, social consequences, and criminal justice outcomes are often intertwined.

We must also *begin developing critical thinking and analytical skills*. If we do not first ask the right questions, our solutions, no matter how well intended and efficient, simply add to our difficulties. Critical thinking and analytical skills help to distinguish concepts such as justice and liberty from principles such as "the ends do not justify the means." These skills encourage openness and perseverance rather than blind acceptance and obedience based on ignorance.

By developing these skills, we realize our third goal, *becoming more personally responsible*. Before we can become more responsible, we must increase our ability to respond. As we persevere in an open exploration and search for the truth regarding moral and ethical issues, we will feel more empowered and have more hope in the future.

The fourth goal in ethics education is *recognizing how criminal justice is engaged in a process of coercion*. Criminal justice is largely about forcing people to do things they do not want to do. Having the authority to be coercive, and the discretionary nature of such authority, creates the potential for corruption and abuse.

Goal five of our exploration concerns what Parker Palmer refers to as *developing wholesight*. Wholesight creates a vision in which our minds and hearts—our thinking and feeling—work together for the common good as we explore the ethical and moral issues we as individuals and members of a community face.

Chapter 2

Utilitarian and Deontological Approaches to Criminal Justice Ethics

by Jeffrey Gold

Key Concepts

categorical imperative	Immanuel Kant
consequentialism	normative ethics
deontology	universalizability
hypothetical imperative	utilitarian calculus
John Stuart Mill	utilitarianism

Introduction

There are some factors that seem to distinguish the moral decisions of criminal justice agents from other professions. First, criminal justice decisions are made on behalf of society as a whole; second, the decisions made are not just incidentally, but are primarily, moral decisions. When the police officer decides to arrest someone, or when a judge gives a suspended sentence, the decisions are primarily moral ones.

It is important that we view issues in criminal justice from the larger framework of ethics and morality. It would be a mistake to assume that criminal justice issues emerge outside of the larger social and ethical context of our culture.

This chapter explores the study of two major philosophical theories in the field of normative ethics: *utilitarianism* and *deontology*. Normative ethics is the study of right and wrong. These two standard ethical theories establish a foundation by which criminal justice issues are examined.

Utilitarianism

Utilitarianism is classified as a consequentialist ethical theory. In other words, we judge the morality of an action in terms of the consequences or results of that action. Cheating, stealing, and murder are all wrong because they produce bad or harmful consequences. Charity and benevolence are good because they produce something beneficial. The morality of an action is determined by the consequences of that action. Actions that are moral produce good consequences; actions that are immoral produce bad consequences. Actions have consequences for many different people. According to John Stuart Mill, the fundamental good that all humans seek is happiness. Mill's view is that all people desire happiness and everything else they desire is either a part of happiness or a means to happiness. Happiness is identified with pleasure according to Mill.

Because utilitarianism holds that we should produce happiness or pleasure, whose happiness or pleasure should be considered? The utilitarians' answer to this is that we should consider all parties influenced by the action, and calculate the pain and pleasure of everyone who is affected. The greatest good for the greatest number creates the context for community. The proportionality of pain and pleasure must be judged in this context.

When calculating the amount of pleasure and pain produced by an action, many factors are relevant. First of all, we must consider the intensity or strength of the pleasure or pain. Then we must consider the duration of the pleasure or pain. In addition, we must consider the long-term consequences of an action. Finally, we must consider the probability or likelihood that our actions will produce the outcomes or consequences we intend.

Deontological Ethics

Some people say that a police officer has a *duty* to issue a ticket regardless of the consequences. This directs us to our second moral theory: *deontological ethics*. Deontology is the study of duty. Deontologists argue that human beings sometimes have a duty to perform certain actions regardless of the consequences. Police officers have a duty to issue tickets even when it does not produce the greatest good for the greatest number.

Perhaps the most famous deontologist is Immanuel Kant. Kant believed that the consequentialist theory missed something crucial to ethics by neglecting the concept of duty as well as a more basic morality, a good will or the intention to do what is right. In other words, the key to morality is human will or intention, not consequences. However, Kant draws a distinction between actions that are merely in accordance with duty and actions that are taken for the sake of duty. He holds that only those actions that are taken for the sake of duty have moral worth.

Kant calls the fundamental principle of morality "the categorical imperative." It tells us what we ought to do. The categorical imperative is unhypothetical, no "ifs" whatsoever. Just do it! You ought to behave morally, period. The categorical imperative commands absolutely and unconditionally.

What is the categorical imperative? We will focus on two formulations. The first focuses on a basic concept of ethics called "universalizability"—that for my action to be morally justified, I must be able to see that anyone in relatively similar circumstances would act the same way. Morality involves fairness or equality—a willingness to treat everyone the same way. Kant's idea is that you should do only what you are willing to permit anyone else to do.

The next formulation focuses on the fact that human beings have intrinsic value (that is, value in and of themselves). Human beings should always be treated with reverence, and never treated as mere things.

To summarize, let us contrast deontological ethics with utilitarianism ethics.

Utilitarianism is a consequentialist moral theory. We must weigh the positive results of our actions against the negative results in deciding what to do. Deontology is the study of duty. The deontologist believes the key to morality is human will or intention, not consequences. This chapter attempts to explain how the two theories approach ethical issues in criminal justice.

Justice and Duty

Treating people as ends and producing the greatest amount of happiness both seem to be credible guides to the moral life. Nonetheless, both theories seem to have trouble with a certain range of cases. Utilitarianism seems to have difficulty with cases of injustice, and deontology seems to have no way to handle cases of conflicting duties. In this section, we attempt to explore the weaker points of both theories and propose an ethic to handle their difficulties.

According to utilitarianism, an action is moral when it produces the greatest amount of happiness for the greatest number of people. A problem arises when the greatest happiness is achieved at the expense of a few. If we were to follow a utilitarian calculus, the suffering of a few—even intense suffering—would be outweighed by the pleasure of a large enough majority. Most of us, though, believe that slavery and oppression are wrong regardless of the amount of pleasure experienced by the oppressing class. It is always wrong to treat someone as a mere means to one's own ends. It is simply unjust to mistreat anyone in order to benefit others.

Deontology also has its problems. Kant speaks extensively of duty. However, he seems to have no way to deal with cases of conflicting duties. Therefore, it appears that Kant's theory is weak where Mill's is strong, and vice versa. The utilitarian calculus gives us a method of determining what to do in cases of conflicting duties. An action ought to be taken in a situation if and only if: (1) doing the action (a) treats as mere means as few people as possible in the situation, and (b) treats as ends as many people as is consistent with (a); and (2) taking the action in the situation brings about as much overall happiness as is consistent with (1). This integrated approach avoids the problem of enslaving a few because such an act would violate (1). It also avoids the problem of conflicting duties because (2) provides a way of deciding what to do when we are faced with a conflict of duties.

Chapter 3

Peacemaking, Justice, and Ethics

by Michael C. Braswell & Jeffrey Gold

Key Concepts

> caring
> connectedness
> mindfulness
> peacemaking

Introduction

The evolution of legal and social justice in America often has found itself pulled between the rehabilitation and punishment agendas. Ancient traditions emphasize the value and usefulness of suffering and service, which are often de-emphasized or nonexistent in new-age movements. Peacemaking, as evolved from ancient spiritual and wisdom traditions, has included the possibility of mercy and compassion within the framework of justice. As explained in this chapter, peacemaking has three themes: (1) connectedness, (2) care, and (3) mindfulness.

Connectedness

Philosophers suggest that humans are not simply isolated individuals, but each one of us is integrally "connected" and bonded to other human beings and the environment—an environment that not only includes the outer physical environment but our inner psychological and spiritual environment as well. It has been suggested that everybody and everything in the universe is connected, but most of us just cannot see the "glue." An important aspect of connectedness is looking within, taking personal responsibility, and acting in a more responsible way. Because we are connected to everyone and everything around us, our actions affect those who are connected to us even when we cannot see the connections. In other words, what goes around comes around.

Caring

One might say that professional and academic ethics have been discussed largely in the language of the masculine or the father, in principles and propositions, in terms such as justification, fairness, and justice. The feminine perspective or mother's voice has often been silent. Human caring and the memory of caring and being cared for have not received attention except primarily as outcomes of ethical behavior. The point is that ethical caring is ultimately grounded in natural caring (for example, the natural caring a mother has for her child).

Mindfulness

Mindfulness allows us to experience a more transcendent sense of awareness. Mindfulness allows us to be fully present and aware of what is immediate. It also allows us to become more aware of the larger picture both in terms of needs and possibilities. A strategy or process that can help us become more mindful is meditation. Meditation can help clear the mind and make it stronger. This awareness can become a kind of awakening, encouraging us to make more informed and ethical decisions about the way we conduct our lives.

Conclusion

If we choose to become more peaceful through connectedness, caring, and mindfulness, it should follow that as persons and criminal justice professionals we will act more morally and ethically. For peacemaking to work, we must examine it on the personal level first. Peacemaking offers us a vision of hope grounded in the reality of which we are a part.

Chapter 4

Learning Police Ethics

by Lawrence Sherman

Key Concepts

apologia	moral career
contingencies	moral experience
ethics	morals
metamorphosis	occupational career

Introduction

The two ways to learn police ethics are: (1) learning on the job under pressure; and (2) learning police ethics in an environment free from such pressures. The second, less common, way of learning police ethics also allows the police officer to be more objective and have a more clear and open mind.

Learning New Jobs

Every new job starts with a learning process called socialization. The socialization process serves to encourage "rookies" to adopt and adapt to the rules, values, and attitudes of veteran officers. In many instances, informal rules and attitudes conflict with the formal or official rules and attitudes to which the general society expects police officers to adhere. Such a dilemma puts a rookie in the middle and poses the question: Which set of rules should I follow?

Regardless of the situation a rookie faces, reactions to the learning process can be described as his or her *moral career*—how he or she changes in terms of morality and the ethics of behavior. The police officer's moral career is closely connected to the occupational career that addresses the stages of growth and development in becoming a police officer.

Becoming a Police Officer

The four major stages or phases in the career of any person joining an occupation are:

1. The person's choice of occupation.
2. The introduction of that person to the occupation.
3. The person's first encounter with doing the occupation's work.
4. The metamorphosis into becoming a full-fledged member of the occupation

I. Choice

The three aspects of the choice to become a police officer are:

1. The kind of person who makes the choice.
2. The reason the choice is made and the motivations for doing police work.
3. The methods people most use as police officers.

It seems that police work attracts the sons and daughters of successful tradespeople and civil servants (especially police). A reasonable salary, job security, and the prestige of police work may represent an improvement over their parents' socioeconomic position. Police applicants often perceive police work as an exciting adventure and a chance to make a positive difference in their communities. Since the 1980s, the selection process has become highly selective and, as a result, successful applicants may often feel they have been included in an elite group of highly qualified people.

II. Introduction

New police officers are quickly introduced to folklore that emphasizes how things cannot be done "by the book" and how it is often necessary to "bend the rules." Police typically use "war stories"—anecdotes about on-the-job policing—to communicate the history and values of the department.

III. Encounter

When confronted with real police work, the rookie experiences a kind of "reality shock." Rookies often find themselves caught between unreasonable citizen demands and the job they have to do.

IV. *Metamorphosis*

The result of encounters with the public can encourage a change, a metamorphosis in the rookie's self-conception as a "cop." Police officers tend to become dependent upon other police officers for survival and support. Some assumptions that new police officers come to accept are: (1) loyalty to colleagues is essential for survival; (2) most of the public is the enemy; and (3) police administrators are not to be trusted. By the time the metamorphosis has been completed, most of these new values have been learned by the new officers.

Content of Police Values Teachings

Following are some of the primary values that police officers are taught:

1. Discretion A: Decisions about whether to enforce the law, in any but the most serious cases, should be guided by both what the law says and who the suspect is.

2. Discretion B: Disrespect for police authority is a serious offense that should always be punished with an arrest or the use of force.

3. Force: Police officers should never hesitate to use physical or deadly force against people who "deserve it" or when it can be an effective way of solving a crime.

4. Due Process: Due process is only a means of protecting criminals at the expense of the law-abiding and should be ignored whenever it is safe to do so.

5. Truth: Lying and deception are an essential part of the police job, and even perjury should be used if it is necessary to protect yourself or get a conviction of a "bad guy."

6. Time: You cannot go fast enough to chase a car thief or traffic violator nor slow enough to get to a 'garbage' call; and when there are no calls for service, your time is your own.

7. Rewards: Police do very dangerous work for low wages, so it is proper to take any extra rewards the public wants to give them, like free meals, Christmas gifts, or even regular monthly payments for special treatment.

8. Loyalty: The paramount duty is to protect your fellow officers at all costs, as they would protect you, even though you may have to risk your own career or your own life to do it.

The Rising Value Conflicts

There may be a number of reasons why traditional police values have begun to break down, including the diversity of individuals joining police agencies as well as the rise in investigative journalism.

The Police Officer's Moral Career

There are four main aspects of moral careers in general that are directly relevant to police officers:

1. Contingencies the officer confronts.
2. Moral experiences undergone in confronting these contingencies.
3. Apologia, the explanation for changing ethical principles.
4. Stages of moral change.

Contingencies

Contingencies that shape and influence the moral careers of police officers include all social pressures officers have to face to behave one way rather than another. Some contingencies will encourage ethical behavior while others will encourage unethical actions.

Moral Experience

The moral experience is a major crossroads point at which a decision must be made. The moral experience can be an agonizing decision about which values to follow or not follow. One choice is to go along with the corrupt behavior and do nothing, and another is to try to escape from the moral dilemma. A third option is to choose to leave police work altogether, and a final option would be to try to fight against the corrupt or unethical practice. Not all moral experiences are prompted by criminal acts. For example, racist jokes or language may also prompt a moral experience.

Apologia

In an attempt to resolve feelings of conflict between what they think they should have done and what they actually have done, many police officers invent or adopt an acceptable explanation for their behavior, called an apologia. The progression from one apologia to another makes up the stages of moral change in a police officer.

Stages

Officers progress, become stagnant, or regress in the moral stages of their career. Some police officers evolve into more serious stages of unethical conduct as they become more experienced. The movement from one stage to another makes up an officer's moral career in police work. Ethically speaking, police officers become better, worse, or stay the same.

Conclusion: Learning Ethics Differently

Morality is not black and white; it has many gray areas. Police officers, just as civilians, learn ethics and morality in different ways. Police issues regarding ethics are not always clear cut. Learning ethics can be a complex and perplexing process.

Chapter 5

The Ethics of Deceptive Interrogation

by Jerome H. Skolnick & Richard A. Leo

Key Concepts

fabricated evidence   *Miranda v. Arizona*
Fourteenth Amendment   role playing
interrogation   slippery slope argument
interview   Wickersham Report

Introduction

Investigative and interrogatory lying are justifiable on utilitarian crime control grounds. While physical coercion during the interrogation phase is quite rare in the United States, psychological persuasion and manipulation are used extensively in order to elicit "voluntary" confessions. Admission of guilt by coercion has traditionally involved: (1) denial of food or sleep, (2) threats of harm or punishment, (3) lengthy/incommunicado interrogation, (4) psychological pressure, (5) promises of leniency, and (6) physical force.

The Jurisprudence of Interrogation

The law of confessions is governed by the Fifth, Sixth, and Fourteenth Amendments. Three principles involved in the law of confessions include: (1) the truth-finding rationale (goal of reliability), (2) the substantive due process/fairness rationale (goal of system's integrity), and (3) the deterrence principle (proscribes offense or lawless police conduct). Implementation of the *Miranda v. Arizona* (1966) decision safeguards the defendant's Fifth Amendment right against compulsion to testify. In light of *Miranda*, police must advise a suspect of the right to remain silent and the right to an attorney. Before a custodial interrogation can legally commence, the suspect must "voluntarily, knowingly, and intelligently" have waived these rights.

Typology of Interrogatory Deception

The following are examples of the types of deception police may carry out at the interrogation:

1. Interrogation versus interview—a tactic used by police to circumvent *Miranda* by turning the custodial interrogation into a noncustodial interview; the suspect is free to leave questioning and acknowledges that he or she is voluntarily answering questions
2. *Miranda* warnings—recite the rights specified by *Miranda* in an unimportant, monotone style to downplay the importance of its contents
3. Misrepresent the nature or seriousness of the offense
4. Role-playing—good cop/bad cop
5. Misrepresenting (downplaying) the moral seriousness of the offenses
6. The use of promises
7. Misrepresentation of identity (of officers)
8. Fabricated evidence
   a. An accomplice has testified against the offender
   b. The physical evidence confirms guilt
   c. Creation of an eyewitness
   d. Stage a line-up
   e. Have suspect take polygraph

The Consequence of Deception

Coercion and deceptive interrogations can lead to false confessions that undermine the concept of due process. Deception on behalf of the police can also lead to greater skepticism and criticism of police officers. It also reduces police effectiveness as controllers of crime.

Independent Exercise

Explain how each of the following court cases was significant to the jurisprudence of interrogation:

Arizona v. Fulminate (1991)
Brown v. Mississippi (1936)
Colorado v. Spring (1987)
Florida v. Cayward (1989)
Frazier v. Cupp (1969)
Illinois v. Perkins (1990)
Miller v. Fenton (1986)
Moran v. Burbine (1986)
People v. Adams (1983)

Chapter 6

Ethical Dilemmas in Police Work

by Joycelyn Pollock & Ronald Becker

Key Concepts

discretion	loyalty
duty	police ethics
gratuities	utilitarianism

Introduction

Teaching ethics in criminal justice curricula, especially police ethics, is becoming an important part of the criminal justice program. This brings up the issue of where such ethics be taught—the college classroom or the police academy? However, there is an increasing recognition that both settings are important. Another important issue concerns whether teaching ethics should be conducted in an academy recruit class or as part of in-service training. Again, the answer is perhaps both settings.

John Kleinig suggests that police ethics is particularly relevant because of the number of issues involved such as the discretionary nature of policing, police authority, crisis situations, and peer pressure. The goals of police training typically involve all aspects of how to perform tasks related to the job. Such tasks include com-munication skills, multicultural understandings, and training in child abuse and the "battered woman's syndrome."

Ethical dilemmas for police officers can be extracted from newspapers, textbooks, and articles. The literature identifies a variety of ethical dilemmas including the following issues: gratuities, corruption, bribery, whistle-blowing and loyalty, undercover tactics, the use of deception, discretion, sleeping, sex, misfeasance, deadly force, and brutality. One might assume that these issues are the most problematic ethical issues in police work because they are the ones primarily addressed in the literature. However, officers themselves may not perceive these issues as the most problematic.

Barker found that officers believed that sleeping on duty and engaging in sex while on duty were the most frequent forms of misconduct, and they were also rated as relatively less serious than other forms of unethical behavior. In the study, police officers ranked offenses from most serious to least serious: drinking on duty, police perjury, sleeping on duty, sex on duty, and brutality.

Each of the authors taught ethics to police officers. They used ethical dilemmas and problem situations turned in by class participants as the basis for one-half of the course content. First, the instructor defined the term *ethical dilemma* as a situation in which: (1) the officer did now know what was the right choice of action; (2) the course of action that he or she considered right was difficult to do; or (3) what was identified as the wrong course of action was very tempting. The officers in each class were asked to write down a difficult ethical dilemma or problem they had faced. It is not clear whether officers reported ethical dilemmas according to frequency or seriousness or for some other reason.

Another exercise was to have officers write their own code of ethics in an abbreviated and simple manner. Police officers identified five common elements: (1) legality (enforcing and upholding the law); (2) service (protecting and serving the public); (3) honesty and integrity; (4) loyalty; and (5) the golden rule (respect for others). The five elements that officers viewed as important to a code of ethics were also tied to the dilemmas they identified. Legality can be discussed in terms of discretion. Service is relevant to duty issues. Honesty is related to whistle-blowing and loyalty issues as well as temptations to take money from a crime scene or accepting a bribe. Finally, the golden rule is related to incidents in which it is difficult to keep one's temper. These five elements comprise four categories of dilemmas: (1) discretion, (2) duty, (3) honesty, and (4) loyalty.

Discretion

Discretion can be defined as the ability and power to make a choice of one kind or another. All ethical dilemmas involve making choices. Examples of police discretion include whether to arrest, whether to ticket, and what to do when faced with an altercation.

Another category of discretion involves situations in which no clear policy may be apparent, such as in family disputes. Here, the officer may want to do the right thing, but may not be sure what the right thing is. For most officers in such a case, it may not necessarily be a question of doing something wrong but rather of finding the best solution to a difficult problem.

The last problem situation—domestic disputes—is the single most frequent type of instance identified in this category. Typically, boyfriends wanted girlfriends removed, girlfriends wanted boyfriends removed, parents wanted children removed, and spouses wanted spouses removed. Police officers expressed frustration in having to deal with what are essentially difficult, often unsolvable, interpersonal problems.

Duty

Duty involves incidents in which there is a real question concerning what exactly is the duty of the police officer in a certain situation. Duty issues may also involve situations in which the officer knows that the job requires a particular action, but feels that the action is either inconvenient or a waste of time. Some police officers believe that they have a duty or obligation to help the poor and homeless find shelter; other officers see their job as being free from such responsibilities.

The other type of duty dilemma is more straightforward. Here, the officer knows there is a specific duty to perform. An example would be driving by the scene of an accident or avoiding it altogether because it occurs at the end of a shift. Another duty-related issue arose concerning the risk of contracting AIDS due to possible contact with injured suspects or victims. Finally, there were other miscellaneous duty issues, all concerned with the general idea of using regular work hours to conduct personal business.

In discussing duty issues, participants learned that not all police officers view duty in the same way. It is necessary to apply an ethical framework analysis that helps officers understand that while their position may be legal, and justifiable to some extent, it may still be unethical.

Honesty

Under this topic, officers submitted dilemmas involving self-protection or enrichment, honesty versus the need to make an arrest, and bribery. Many officers reported situations in which they were confronted with temptations of money or other goods. While many officers would feel that it was a minor indiscretion at best to keep $20, at some point as the amount of "found" money increased, individual officers perceived keeping it as being unethical.

Another type of dilemma involved officers trying to cover up their own wrongdoing by lying or not coming forward when they committed minor unethical or illegal acts. Police officers also raised the issue of whether to tell the truth and lose (or risk losing) an arrest or whether to misrepresent facts to make an arrest. Bribery is also a form of dishonesty. It can be defined as a reward for doing something illegal or for not doing something that is required, such as taking money in exchange for not issuing a speeding ticket.

Loyalty

In a problem situation involving loyalty, the consideration of "whistle-blowing" forced officers to decide what to do when faced with the wrongdoing of other police officers. Officers' experiences ran the gamut from seeing relatively minor offenses to observing very serious violations. An example would be whether to report a fellow officer who used what was considered excessive force. Covering up for another officer in the 1990s is more risky than ever before because of the possibility of individual civil liability, and it may be that fewer officers are willing to draw the "blue curtain." Of course, reporting a fellow officer because he or she did something wrong about which only the reporting officer knows and telling the truth in an official investigation in order to avoid being disciplined represent very different types of ethical decisionmaking.

Conclusion

Some decisions have little or no ethical rationale supporting them. In addition, some rationales for actions can only be described as primarily self-serving. Officers are seldom forced to present ethical rationales for their decisions. Some do not like the experience. This chapter presents the premise that the best ethics course for police officers is one that is relevant to them. One way to achieve that is to utilize their own dilemmas. Police officers need the tools to identify and resolve their own ethical dilemmas in the course of their work.

Chapter 7

Police Ethics, Legal Proselytism, and the Social Order: Paving the Path to Misconduct

by Victor E. Kappeler & Gary W. Potter

Key Concepts

appeals to higher loyalties	denial of responsibility
collective responsibility	denial of the victim
condemnation of the condemners	police use of force
denial of injury	techniques of neutralization

Introduction

Policing is an occupation with many unique features. Police must be versatile. They often must respond to citizens in times of need and tragedy. Police hold positions of public trust and are expected to not take advantage of people in their time of need. However, police also must assist people with non-emergency requests. Police perform many different functions within their communities. Officers are frequently role models. Police are often in contact with children and young adults. They are the gatekeepers of the justice system and symbolize our government. Police also have been entrusted with the power to detain and arrest persons, to search and seize property, and to use force. Because police have the ability to use and misuse force, they represent one of the greatest potential threats to rights and liberties. There is much potential for corruption and abuse in the policing field. In sum, policing's unique features make professional ethics extremely important in this occupation.

The Path to Unethical Conduct

A way of thinking (i.e., worldview), attitudes, and beliefs often precede behavior, action, and conduct. How police view themselves, their careers, and the world around them sets the stage for unethical conduct. Police often stereotype people into roles and see the world in the simple terms of good versus evil. Police may also come to view their work as integral to social cohesion and order. For many officers, policing is not just about what they do, but it becomes who they are.

Legally Permissible but Unethical Conduct

In most police training academies, the law is presented as an unquestionable system of rights and wrongs. The law is not something to be challenged, it is to be mastered as the foundation for action. Law is seen as the equivalent of goodness. However, the law is often written and can be interpreted in ways that give the police sufficient latitude to engage in unethical conduct in their pursuit of different objectives. Due to the ambiguity of the law and the police's situational interpretation of these legal mandates, the law itself contributes to unethical conduct. Some officers may come to believe that masterful police work often involves manipulation and situational application of the law to achieve enforcement objectives.

Socially Situating Unethical Behavior

Police may behave unethically due to their worldview, the way police work is legally and perceptually framed, and the manner in which their actions are socially situated. Police officers draw upon preconstructed frames of reference to excuse, justify, and rationalize a variety of unethical behaviors. Police may use techniques of neutralization to maintain a positive self-image even when they have engaged in misconduct. These coping mechanisms may include denial of responsibility, denial of injury, denial of the victim, condemnation of the condemners, and appeals to higher loyalties.

Collective Responsibility for Unethical Police Conduct

Elements in society may contribute to unethical police conduct as well. The media presents a view of police as holding back a tide of criminality. Politicians always appear pro-police. These factors add to a worldview of police work as always good, effective, and successful at any cost.

Chapter 8

Pure Legal Advocates and Moral Agents: Two Concepts of a Lawyer in an Adversary System

by Elliot D. Cohen

Key Concepts

> moral agent
> moral autonomy
> moral courage
> moral respectability
> pure legal advocate

Introduction

A morally good person is someone who has developed morally desirable traits of character. Such a person would be inclined to act, think, and feel in certain ways that are morally desirable. For example, a morally good person may have the following characteristics: fairness, truthfulness, moral courage, respectfulness, financial responsibility, benevolence, trustworthiness, and moral autonomy.

The Pure Legal Advocate Concept

One way to define what a lawyer is has to do with performing as the client's legal advocate. Such a lawyer might be considered a pure legal advocate. An advocate focuses on one person: his or her client. The duty of the pure legal advocate is to win the case for the client by all means at his or her disposal, including those involving difficulties for other persons or for himself or herself. A good lawyer is one who is a skilled legal technician, who can manipulate rules of law to the advantage of his or her client's legal interests. Such a lawyer may feel required to do certain things for his or her client that would ordinarily be regarded as being morally questionable or objectionable.

There are several moral shortcomings of the pure legal advocate model. First, to some extent, a lawyer who is a pure legal advocate would not always be a just person. Such a lawyer may find it necessary to violate the moral rights of individuals while staying within the legal limits in order to advance the legal gains. Second, pure legal advocates would not appear to meet the standards of truthfulness. Third, the pure legal advocate would not support moral courage. Fourth, the pure legal advocate would not support liberality. Fifth, the pure legal advocate would not necessarily be a benevolent person. Sixth, the pure legal advocate would ignore any obligation other than the interests of his or her client. And lastly, moral autonomy would not be an issue with a pure legal advocate.

The Moral Agent Concept

The moral agent concept suggests that a good lawyer is a morally good person—one who is an effective legal advocate and a moral agent. The moral agent concept suggests that a good lawyer is effective in *morally* as well as legally advocating his or her client's cause. The moral agent would adhere to several "natural laws" of the legal practice:

1. Treat others as ends in themselves and not as mere means to winning cases.
2. Treat clients and other professional relations who are relatively similar in a similar fashion.
3. Do not deliberately engage in behavior apt to deceive the court as to the truth.
4. Be willing, if necessary, to make reasonable personal sacrifices—of time, money, popularity, and so on—for what you believe to be a morally good cause.
5. Do not give money to, or accept money from, clients for wrongful purposes or in wrongful amounts.
6. Avoid harming others in the process of representing your client.
7. Be loyal to your client and do not betray his or her confidences.
8. Make your own moral decisions to the best of your ability and act consistently.

The Moral Agent Concept and the ABA

The American Bar Association (ABA) recognizes several corollaries of their general principles (found in the ABA Code). These include individual justice, distributive justice, truthfulness, moral courage, liberality, nonmalevolence, and trustworthiness. These qualities are more consistent with the idea of a moral agent than that of a pure legal advocate. The revised Model Rules of Professional Conduct, specified by the ABA, are more obligatory than previously presented. This trend is more consistent with the moral agent concept.

Chapter 9

Why Prosecutors Misbehave

by Bennett L. Gershman

Key Concepts

courtroom misconduct
forensic misconduct
harmless error doctrine
oral advocacy
prosecutorial misconduct

Introduction

The primary interest of the prosecutor is not only to win the case but that justice shall be done. The prosecutor is the servant of the law. Courtroom misconduct includes types of misconduct that involve efforts to influence or sway the jury through various types of improper or inadmissible evidence. Foren-sic misconduct has been explained as any effort by the prosecutor to keep the jury from making its determination of guilt or innocence by considering the legally admitted evidence in the manner prescribed by law.

Why Misconduct Occurs

The main reason that courtroom misconduct occurs is that it works. For example, the opening statement is very crucial. Research indicates that a strong opening statement by the prosecutor will influence the jury throughout the entire trial. Research also suggests that whichever side (prosecution or defense) raises arguments with the substantive case of the other, the jury will be more inclined to believe the critical team. Also, stricken evidence may influence the jury's verdict. Finally, because the prosecutor represents the state, he or she is often perceived as the "good guy."

Why Misconduct Continues

One of the most fundamental reasons for the continued presence of prosecutorial misconduct is the "harmless error doctrine." The practical objective of the harmless error doctrine is to utilize judicial resources more effectively by enabling appellate courts to correct prejudicial error without becoming bogged down in harmless error. The problem is that the stronger the prosecutor's case, the more misconduct he or she can commit without being reversed. It is clear that, by deciding as they do, courts provide little discouragement to prosecutors who believe that they do not have to be as careful about their conduct when they have a strong case. Perhaps the ultimate reason that prosecutorial conduct persists is that prosecutors are not personally liable for their misconduct. Allowing prosecutors to be completely shielded from civil liability in the event of misconduct provides little deterrent to courtroom misconduct.

Chapter 10

Criminal Sentencing:
Honesty, Prediction, Discrimination, and Ethics

by Lawrence F. Travis III

Key Concepts

desert	prediction
deterrence	punishment
false negative	sentencing
false positive	treatment
incapacitation	utilitarianism

Introduction

Punishment is the traditional response to criminal offenses. To some extent, criminal punishment is returning harm to an offender for harm the offender caused the victim. However, we are also taught that two wrongs don't make a right. This dilemma often results in moral or ethical conflict. Because ethics is the study of right and wrong, punishment and sentencing should be a prime area of focus for moral inquiry. By violating the law, the offender has wronged society; and by punishing, society may arguably "wrong" the offender.

The Purpose of Criminal Punishment

When, whom, and how we punish depends on why we punish. Traditionally, four reasons for punishment have been advanced: (1) deterrence, (2) incapacitation, (3) treatment, and (4) desert. Deterrence is based on a rational conception of human agency guided by a pleasure principle that enables us to avoid things that may cause pain. Deterrence works on general and specific levels. General deterrence occurs when the offender is punished in way that will discourage others from committing that crime. Specific deterrence occurs when the punishment is designed to convince a particular or specific offender not to commit future crimes. For punishment to deter, three conditions must be met: (1) severity, (2) certainty, and (3) swiftness. The first condition entails severity. That is, the punishment must outweigh the pleasure derived from crime. The second condition entails certainty. That is, the punishment must be imposed. Likewise, the punishment must be swift.

The second rationale justifies punishment on the basis of preventing offenders from having the chance to commit new crimes. This concept is known as incapacitation. Given our lack of ability to predict who will commit future crimes, we must "lock up" large numbers of offenders who are not dangerous in order to punish the dangerous offenders.

Treatment is the third rationale for punishment. The primary goal of treatment is to reduce future crimes (offending) by addressing the different factors that influence criminality. These factors include poverty, discrimination, and psychological problems. As with incapacitation, treatment programs are limited by our inability to predict behavior and to design and implement effective therapeutic strategies.

The fourth rationale for punishment involves the concept of desert. Desert is based on the retributive idea that the criminal deserves to be punished as a result of committing an offense. Desert places limits on the degree to which individuals may be punished. Desert also requires that the punishment be proportional to the severity of the crime that has been committed.

Contemporary Ethical Concerns in Sentencing

The first area of concern involving sentencing includes honesty about punishment. Current policies lead to particular mistruths in sentencing. Sentences delivered in court are often very different from the actual time served. Additionally, some states allow inmates to earn "good time." Good time is simply a reduction in the time served. It is based on good behavior while in the institution. Discretionary release also reduces time served. For example, an inmate sentenced to eight years may be paroled after only three. There are several different ways to address honesty in sentencing. First, we could keep offenders incarcerated longer. Second, we could lower the court sentences of offenders to approximate the time they actually will serve. The third approach simply combines the first and second solutions—increasing time served for violent criminals and decreasing time served for nonviolent offenders.

Prediction in punishment is another ethical issue in sentencing. In prediction, a false positive occurs when we inaccurately "diagnose" someone as a threat who is actually benign. A false negative occurs when we inaccurately "diagnose" someone as not being a threat and the person goes on to commit future crimes. A dilemma arises as to the accuracy of our prediction capacities. Whenever we decrease the likelihood of a false positive, we increase our chances of a false negative. Conversely, when we decrease the likelihood of a false negative, we increase the chances of committing a false positive. Another concern involves the dilemma of incapacitating persons for crimes they have not yet committed.

The last area of concern in sentencing deals with discrimination in sentencing. There is research to suggest that females, older adults, whites, and the more affluent receive more lenient sentences than males, minority groups, young adults, and the poor. Sentencing decisions do not rely solely on prior criminal record and criminal justice history. The effects of race, class, and sex may be latent or hidden; in fact, prejudices can exist on a subconscious level as well as a conscious one. The classification of persons into risk groups generates a complex problem that mirrors many of the prejudices in contemporary America.

Chapter 11

Myth that Punishment Can Fit the Crime

by Harold E. Pepinsky & Paul Jesilow

Key Concepts

certainty
punishment
retribution
severity
swiftness

Introduction

Shylock, in Shakespeare's *Merchant of Venice*, contracted to receive a pound of flesh as payment if a borrower defaulted on a loan. When the borrower defaulted, the court ruled in Shylock's favor, and a final judgment was rendered. Shylock was entitled to his pound of flesh, but not one ounce more. If even a single drop of excess blood fell out of the wound, he would violate the agreement and be criminally liable for the harm done. As a result of the court's decision, Shylock was forced to abandon his quest for justice and exercise mercy instead.

When a lawbreaker violates the social contract of a just society, many people believe that the lawbreaker should be punished accordingly. This model of justice is known as the "just deserts" model. Punishment should exactly fit the crime. *Lex talionis* (an eye for an eye) is the classical definition of retribution. However, it is very difficult to assess what punishment will fit which crime. Additionally, there are many factors such as gender, attractiveness, and remorsefulness that influence sentencing and punishment.

Controlling Punishment

To fit the crime, punishment needs to be severe, swift, and certain. If punishment is delayed too long, the connection between it and the offense may become ambiguous and unclear. Retribution is a response to moral outrage about a recent wrongdoing. It seems contradictory to punish someone who has been behaving properly for an extended period of time for an offense that happened long ago. That is a primary reason why statutes of limitation restrict prosecution for all but the most serious crimes.

Criminal justice officials, if required to punish officials more severely, tend to be more careful and selective. If the same officials are required to punish more often, they will temper their severity. If called upon to speed up punishment, officials will tend to be more lenient. Ironically, if these officials are to make swift and sure punishment fit crimes, the crime problem would have to be minimal, if nonexistent, in our society.

Implications for Crime Control

Some supporters of retribution are not concerned with whether punishment prevents crime. Instead, they believe offenders should be punished even if such punishment only offers moral and emotional satisfaction. However, other supporters of retribution believe swift and sure punishment of controlled severity can deter persons from committing a first offense or from committing additional crimes. However, evidence suggests that societies that use extensive and severe punishment continue to have serious problems with crime and violence.

Chapter 12

A Life for a Life?
Opinion and Debate

by Robert Johnson

Key Concepts

> death penalty
> golden rule
> *lex talionis*
> life imprisonment
> retribution

Introduction

Johnson opens the chapter by stating that most Americans support the death penalty for the crime of murder. Most people want murderers to be paid back for their crimes. This is a retributive model of justice, based upon revenge: a life for a life. In the United States there are more than 2,000 persons awaiting execution. Legal appeals are running out for hundreds of condemned prisoners.

Murderers are People, Too

An execution is always a tragic ending to human life. The belief that the person put to death has committed a terrible crime and in some abstract sense may deserve to die does not change this fact. However, many people ignore the tragic side of the death penalty. For many people, executing a murderer is not seen as killing a fellow human being. By executing murderers, we disown them, wash our hands of them, and punish them as only monsters should be punished: violently, with utter disregard for their humanity. However, murderers are dangerously flawed human beings; they are not creatures beyond comprehension or control.

A Killing by Any Other Name

Lex talionis—retaliation in kind, an eye for an eye—is perhaps the most cogent moral principle that can be invoked to support the death penalty for the crime of murder. The death penalty is sometimes referred to as the "law enforcement arm of the golden rule (do unto others as you would have them do unto you)." Delegating the administration of justice to the state was meant to make humankind more civilized, to end blood feuds, and raise our punishments to a level of mature, compassionate discourse. However, the idea that we should kill killers has always had a fairly wide following. One reason why it may be easy to contemplate executing murderers is simply that a killing can be committed discretely by agents of the state. Another reason that murderers are executed with few qualms on the part of the public is that these offenders are readily seen as "monsters." That is, we demonize murderers and label them as "other" than us. Furthermore, it must be noted that execution is a premeditated killing.

Conclusion

When we sentence criminals to prison we demand a painful suspension of their lives, a temporary death until they are deemed worthy of return to the society of the living. A true life sentence should be used as a practical moral alternative to the death penalty, a civilized and civilizing application of the golden rule. A life sentence is a painful punishment, but it can be borne with dignity. A true life sentence would replace execution as our most severe penalty.

A Life for a Life?—Reply (by van de Haag)

Van den Haag questions the validity of each point raised by Johnson in his critique of the death penalty. First, van den Haag asserts that there is no evidence for the lack of empathy among supporters of the death penalty. He also attacks Johnson's conceptualization of humanity. Van den Haag does not see capital punishment as inconsistent with a civilized society. He views execution as a lawful punishment for a crime, not as a premeditated cold-blooded killing. He believes that a death sentence can be borne with dignity.

In conclusion, van den Haag argues that the death penalty is a more suitable penalty for murder than is life imprisonment. He disagrees with Johnson on the possible deterrent effects of the death penalty if it were imposed on a regular basis. He stands by the basic tenet that would-be murderers can best be controlled by the threat of an enforceable death penalty.

Chapter 13

Ethical Issues in Probation, Parole, and Community Corrections

by John T. Whitehead

Key Concepts

>community supervision
>parole
>probation
>whistle-blowing

Introduction

Joan Petersilia of the RAND Corporation authored a report of the effectiveness of probation supervision for felons in California. The report indicated serious problems with felony probation: 65 percent of the felons studied were rearrested within 40 months, and one-third were re-incarcerated. It is not surprising, then, that there is some question as to the effectiveness of community supervision.

There are several frequent observations in response to such negative reports. First, the governmental bodies are unwilling to spend enough money on probation. Second, part of the problem may be due to workers not doing the jobs that they should be doing. Workers may not be living up to the ethical standard of putting in a full day's work for a full day's pay. Third, there is no consensus in criminology as to what forms of rehabilitation work and what do not. Moreover, criminology has yet to provide a unified theory of criminality and offending.

The Mission of Probation and Parole

Traditionally, the mission of probation and parole supervision has been described as some combination of assistance and control, treatment and security, or service and surveillance. The ethical perspective to this mission involves whether offenders are totally free and responsible, and whether society has some obligation to help offenders to some degree. Recent developments in community supervision, such as house arrest, electronic monitoring of offenders, intensive supervision, and calls for the elimination of parole, raise important ethical considerations.

Supervision Fees

Related to the issue of increasing emphasis on surveillance techniques in community supervision is the question of charging probationers and parolees supervision fees. This growing trend in community corrections raises some important ethical considerations. On the one hand, collecting money can detract from the supervision officer's main mission of risk control. Likewise, fees represent a financial burden for many offenders. On the other hand, fees have no negative impact on the collection of restitution orders or the service mission itself. Furthermore, supervision fees are politically attractive.

Ethical Issues in Presentence Investigation

The main ethical issue in presentence investigation appears to be deceptiveness. Officers attempt to establish rapport with defendants during interviews aimed at obtaining information for the reports. The presentence investigation, then, is not really an investigation. Rather, it involves the probation officer's preparation of the defendant for the sentence. Presentence investigation reports provide information useful to probation officers who supervise offenders sentenced to probation. In addition, the reports also convey such information to prison officials for incarcerated defendants. In both instances, important details about the offender's educational background, intelligence, psychological state, work experience, and so forth are available so that correctional officials can plan appropriate intervention strategies. The notion that the presentence report is a hallmark of individualized justice is false.

Whistle-blowing

Making internal complaints outside the department is known as "whistle-blowing." In the context of probation, whistle-blowing involves a five-stage process: (1) internal criticism within a given department of questionable or unethical activity, (2) state of intransigency, (3) external disclosure of unethical activities, (4) organizational reaction, and (5) the aftermath. Probation administrators are often unresponsive to line officers raising ethical questions, and whistle-blowing employees are typically transferred to unimportant assignments.

The Role of the Victim

Victims are involved in several stages of probation and parole. Victims can and should enter into the presentence investigation process. Other related ethical issues involve the idea of restitution. First, we need a reliable and precise way of determining the amount of restitution. Second, we need to decide if factors such as depreciation, market demand, condition, and victim involvement in the crime influence the amount of restitution.

Chapter 14

Restorative Justice, Social Justice, and the Empowerment of Marginalized Populations

by Kay Pranis

Key Concepts

> commitment to the common good
> direct participation
> individual accountability
> social distance
> well-being

Introduction

Restorative justice may be able to advance social justice concerns. In particular, the perspective is sensitive to structural factors, such as racism and poverty, that lead to injustice. This chapter looks at the ways in which restorative justice efforts can address some forms of social inequality.

Principles of Restorative Justice and the Relationship to Social Justice Issues

Well-being and wholeness of all community members are at the heart of social justice concerns. Restorative justice emphasizes the well-being of all community members and recognizes that a community must be responsible to its constituents. A key restorative justice principle involves direct participation. Restorative justice calls for active involvement of victims, offenders, and communities in the justice process. Direct participation is essential to a just social order. Both individual accountability and collective accountability are important in restorative justice. Crime is a failure of responsibility by both the offender and his or her community. The response to crime from a restorative justice perspective involves strengthening relationships and mutual responsibility on all levels. On a community level, those who have been harmed and those who have caused harm must be embraced. A restorative community views the event of a crime as an opportunity to strengthen the community, to deepen understanding, and to build caring relationships.

Restorative Processes: Grassroots Democracy at Work

Majority-rule democracy may ignore the interests of minority groups (even when these groups are protected). Under restorative justice ideas, all legitimate community groups must be heard. In fact, restorative justice encourages a broader view of democracy by involving all citizens in decision-making processes that allow interaction and reflection. Restorative justice decision-making models are consensus-based processes that involve the endorsement of the decision by all parties. The restorative justice movement advances several processes emerging from tribal and ancient cultures. For example, both family group conferencing and the peacemaking circle process use consensus decision making and allow participation from affected parties. Furthermore, restorative justice practices give voice and respect to the most disenfranchised groups in society. The grassroots democratic processes represent significant contributions of restorative justice to the broader social justice movement.

"Personal Problems" as Collective Issues: Creating Spaces for Community Dialogue and Problem-Solving

The restorative justice dialogue includes respectful treatment of all views, deep listening to understand the perspective of others, and acceptance of emotions as valid. Restorative justice creates opportunities to link crimes to larger issues by dealing with those incidents in a contextual way. Community members are encouraged to become involved with resolving crimes. Restorative justice processes are filling a void in community life by bringing people together and facilitating respectful and reflective communication about community issues. In sum, restorative justice increases the sense of community responsibility.

Social Distance: The Enemy of Social Justice

Social distance is the extent to which people do not identify with other members in their community or do not feel connected by common interests or a sense of common fate. Restorative processes such as victim-offender dialogue, family group conferencing, community panels, and peacemaking circles bring people together in a face-to-face manner that reduces social distance.

Commitment to the Common Good: The Ally of Social Justice

The development of restorative processes in communities indicates the existence of a deep untapped reservoir and willingness to help others for the good of all. Social justice concerns are forwarded by increased individual commitment to the common good.

Shifting Power from Professionals to Citizens

Restorative justice calls for a transformation in the relationship between communities and professional systems, returning authority and legitimacy to communities as long as communities honor values of fairness, equity, and due process. This is based on the belief that the dominance of professional responses in criminal justice has deprived communities of important opportunities to gain skills and create healthier communities.

Approaching Social Justice from a Restorative Paradigm: Strategic Differences

Traditional social justice activism is often confrontational. Restorative justice is nonconfrontational, focusing on mutual responsibility and understanding. Restorative justice seeks a common ground among different perspectives. One of the paradoxes of restorative justice, therefore, is that it is a vision of radical change formulated in a gentle way. Restorative justice offers islands of common ground on which previously polarized interests can learn to listen to and respect one another. However, if narrowly conceived, restorative justice will not contribute significantly to social justice. Restorative justice includes the themes of both caring and accountability.

Conclusion

Restorative justice engages people in a discussion of shared values and vision and then provides processes for individual community members to experience the human dimension of those through direct participation in other people's lives. Restorative justice makes our fundamental interdependence explicit. Concern about social justice follows naturally from a recognition of interdependence.

Chapter 15

Keeping an Eye on the Keeper:
Prison Corruption and its Control

by Bernard J. McCarthy

Key Concepts

anticorruption policy	material accommodations
corruption	misfeasance
corruption through default	nonfeasance
corruption through friendship	power accommodations
corruption through reciprocity	status accommodations
malfeasance	Sykes's "pains of imprisonment"

Introduction

Corrupt practices in prison range from acts of theft and pilferage to large-scale criminal operations such as drug trafficking. These forms of correctional corruption may involve inmates and employees inside the prison as well as the general community outside the prison. Corrupt correctional practices undermine respect for the justice system. Corruption may also lead to a breakdown in the control structure of the correctional organization and to the demoralization of correctional workers in institutions and in the community.

Defining Corruption in a Correctional Environment

Corruption is defined more specifically as the "intentional violation of organizational norms" by employees for personal gain, usually of a material nature. Prison corruption occurs when an employee violates organizational rules and regulations for his or her own personal material gain. Before an action can be deemed corrupt, the action must involve individuals who are employees. Also, the offense must violate the formal rules of the organization or agency. Lastly, for an action to be corrupt, the offense must involve an employee receiving some specific, personal material gain for his or her misconduct.

39

Types of Prison Corruption

The review of prison internal affairs case files identified several types of corrupt conduct: theft, trafficking in contraband, embezzlement, misuse of authority, and a residual or miscellaneous category. Misuse of authority involves the intentional use of discretion for personal material gain. This type of corruption is comprised of basic offenses directed against inmates: the acceptance of gratuities or rewards from inmates for special consideration in obtaining normal prison privileges; the acceptance of gratuities for help in obtaining normal prison privileges; the acceptance of gratuities for help in obtaining or protecting illicit prison activities; and the mistreatment or extortion of inmates by staff for personal, material gain.

The Role of Discretion

The different types of corruption involve the misuse or abuse of discretion by correctional staff members. The three forms of discretionary misconduct are: (1) misfeasance, (2) malfeasance, and (3) nonfeasance.

Misfeasance refers to the improper performance of some act that an official may lawfully do. Offenses in this area include the acceptance of gratuities for special privileges or preferential treatment, the selective application of formal rewards and punishments to inmates for money, the sale of paroles or other types of releases, and the use of state resources or property for one's own personal gain.

Malfeasance refers to direct misconduct by a staff member, as opposed to the improper use of legitimate authority. Corrupt practices in this category encompass primarily criminal acts, including theft, embezzlement, trafficking in contraband, and extortion.

Nonfeasance refers to the failure to live up to one's responsibilities or the omission of an act for which one is responsible. The two types of corrupt practices in this area are selectively ignoring inmate violations of institutional or organizational rules, and the failure to report or deter other employees who are involved in corrupt behavior.

Factors Associated with Corruption

Two factors that influence the degree of corruption experienced by a particular governmental agency include: (1) the opportunities for corruption, and (2) the level of incentives to make use of those opportunities. Opportunities for corruption arise from the discretionary authority given by the legislature to correctional officials. Punishment, in the form of withdrawal of privileges, transfers, or various forms of deprivation are used to control inmates. The incentives for employees to engage in corruption may result from structural, organization, individual, or personal factors. Friendships with inmates, reciprocal relationships, and defaults undermine the formal control structure of the prison. The type and quality of staff may also affect prison corruption.

Controlling Corruption

Corruption is a regular and traditional feature of the governmental processes. While corruption can probably never be completely eliminated, there are certain steps that may be implemented to help control or minimize the problem. First, an anti-corruption policy must be developed for each institution. Second, the correctional agency needs to cultivate a proactive approach to detect, investigate, and intervene with corrupt practices. Third, the correctional administration needs to be open to improvement in management practices.

In order to minimize corruption, activities that involve a great degree of discretion should be highly structured and monitored. Improved screening and hiring standards should be implemented to ensure a high-caliber staff. Also, external political pressures should be minimized and dealt with by administration.

Chapter 16

Ethics and Prison: Selected Issues

by John T. Whitehead

Key Concepts

discrimination	privatization
elderly offenders	treatment
prison composition	victimization
prison conditions	

Prison Composition

Only about 27 percent of persons incarcerated are admitted to prison for violent offenses. The majority of people sent to prison are neither violent nor career criminals. At the state level, however, six out of 10 prisoners are serving sentences for burglary or a violent offense. The debate about who should go to prison is influenced by politics that fail to consider all of the information. Critics of prisons overemphasize the composition; proponents oversell the alleged benefits.

Discrimination in Sentencing

The problem of racial discrimination is a pressing problem in corrections in the United States. The overrepresentation of African-Americans in prison is a pervasive problem spanning more than 50 years. Although African-Americans comprise about 12 percent of the overall U.S. population, they compose about 34 percent of the prison population. The new drug laws that target crack cocaine are perceived by many simply to enhance the racial disparity in prison. This is a contentious subject that requires more research on the systemic effects of drug law enforcement in our culture.

Prison Conditions

The popular sentiment toward prison conditions calls for a tough prison system without television, recreation facilities, or athletic equipment. Some proponents argue for an increased workload for inmates to serve as punishment. However, there are some voices that believe that prison is already a painful punishment as it is. The deprivation of freedom, autonomy, possessions, security, and heterosexual contact should serve as ample punishment.

Treatment Programs

Rehabilitation has been routinely provided throughout the U.S. prison system. However, many conservatives simply want to provide punishment to the offenders and nothing else. Most prisoners are in dire need of some basic services, such as education. Many have drug or alcohol problems. Some have psychological problems as well. Services to offenders can reduce recidivism when the inmate is released.

Safety in Prison

Victimization occurs within the prison institution. An inmate can be physically or sexually assaulted by another inmate or a guard. Studies differ in actual percentages reported. The ethical mandate here is to make all prisons safe and lawful—even the so-called "undeserving" should have this minimal guarantee.

Elderly Prisoners

Given the changes in sentencing in the past several years, it is likely that prison officials will see increasingly large numbers of prisoners in their sixties, seventies, and eighties. As the prisoners become elderly, many of them will be of no danger to society. The costs of keeping elderly persons incarcerated may become overwhelming.

Women in Prison

Women compose a small proportion of the incarcerated population of the United States. There are fewer women's prisons with fewer treatment programs. Moreover, the discipline women prisoners receive can be authoritarian. The ethical question here addresses the gender inequality that overlaps into prison.

Privatization

Generally, privatization of prisons is argued from an economic perspective. Competition should make private prisons more efficient, accountable, and effective. The ethical problem here involves whether it is appropriate for the government to relinquish control of prisoners to private business. Another related ethical problem includes whether businesses should make a profit at the expense of human suffering. The responsibilities of the private business to the inmates would need to be very clear.

Chapter 17

Crime, Criminals, and Crime Control Policy Myths

by Robert M. Bohm

Key Concepts

crime control myths
crime myths
criminal myths
undesirable consequences

Crime Myths

Myths about crime depend upon one's definition of crime. Historically, the label of crime has been applied to a large and often unrelated number of behaviors. Legal definitions are somewhat arbitrary and appear to depend largely on the interests of the dominant groups in society. All definitions of crime seem to include actions or inactions that could be excluded, and exclude actions or inactions that could be included. Some myths are generated by the discrepancies in the definitions of crimes. However, some myths shape our conceptions of crime and criminality.

The myth that white-collar crime (corporate crime) is nonviolent certainly influences our perceptions. Seldom do we use the word "murder" to describe the loss of life due to unnecessary surgery or cancer caused by environmental toxic waste. Another myth regarding legal definitions of crimes is the assumption that all laws are enforced equitably. Just as there is a bias in the definition of crime, there is a similar bias in the enforcement of law. Another myth that deflects the inadequacy of law enforcement is that regulatory agencies can prevent or regulate white-collar crime. These two problems are at the center of the myth of crime: the definition and the enforcement problem.

There are several other important crime myths in our culture. For example, we believe that crime in America is primarily violent. Likewise, we believe that crime is increasing in our society. The belief that crime is an inevitable result of complex, populous, and industrialized societies is also a common myth.

Criminal Myths

A number of myths also reflect popular beliefs regarding criminals. For example, one myth contends that some groups are more law-abiding than others. However, research suggests that more than 90 percent of all Americans have committed some crime for which they could have been sent to jail. The myth seems credible because the crimes of some (e.g., corporate officials) are not easily detected, or there is not as much effort exerted detecting them. Another myth is that most crime is committed by poor, young males. Regarding age discrimination, an additional problem with this particular myth is that the crime rate is increasing more rapidly than the number of young people.

Crime Control Policy Myths

One of the basic myths concerning law enforcement is that the police are primarily crime fighters. In fact, only a small amount of police time is devoted to fighting crime. Another myth concerning police is that they always solve crimes. The actual crime clearance rate is probably about 13 percent. Another myth of crime control policy is that if injustices from the criminal justice system are eliminated, then the level of serious crime will decrease. However, this may not have an effect on serious violent crime at all.

The preceding list of myths inform and influence the currently dominant politically conservative, "law and order" ideology that has focused on the following principles: mandatory sentencing, habitual-criminal statutes, increased numbers of police officers, more effective police officers, changes in *Miranda* warnings, preventive detention, changes in plea bargaining, changes in the exclusionary rule, changes in the insanity defense, career criminal programs, prison industries, and capital punishment.

Sources of and Reasons for the Myths

Myths and beliefs about crime, criminals, and crime control policy continue because they serve a variety of interests, including those of the general public, the media, politicians, academic criminologists, criminal justice officials, and social elites. The public contributes to myths about crime because they serve at least three short-term goals: (1) myths offer identities, (2) myths aid comprehension by creating order, and (3) myths help forge common bonds and reinforce a sense of community. However, the general public also tends to overgeneralize from their own experiences, rely on inaccurate communication, utilize atypical information, and lack consciousness.

The media generate a distorted picture of crime. Crime-related television programs have been estimated to account for about one-third of all television entertainment shows. The main reason why the media perpetuate crime myths is that they attract a large viewing audience, which is financially profitable. The media, as well as politicians, use public opinion polls to ascertain what opinions are prevalent at a given time in our country.

Academic criminologists and criminal justice officials are often in the best position to dispel the myths, but there are a number of reasons why they do not. Academic criminologists may find an easier life in academia if they do not challenge erroneous beliefs of the status quo. Criminal justice officials gain employment, larger budgets, order, and solidarity through popular crime mythology. Finally, social elites utilize this mythology to legitimize their social status, construct scapegoats, and redirect dissent from the middle classes to the lower classes.

Chapter 18

The Ford Pinto Case and Beyond:
Assessing Blame

by Francis T. Cullen, William J. Maakestad & Gray Cavender

Key Concepts

> corporate misconduct
> political ethics
> white-collar crime

Introduction

Many citizens have become increasingly aware of the enormous costs incurred by white-collar crime, and that the rich and powerful can exact these harms with relative impunity. The matter has become one of not merely preventing victimization but also of confronting why crime allows "the rich to get richer and the poor to get prison." Public awareness of white-collar crime has reached the point at which the concept has become part of the common vernacular. In this social climate, the behavior of big business has taken on a new meaning. The world of big business was seen to suffer. For example, the case against Ford Motor Company brought by the State of Indiana was a manifestation of the broad movement against white-collar crime—and, in particular, against corporate crime.

Assessing Blame

The deaths of three girls in an automobile accident on August 10, 1978, in Indiana initiated a crusade against the Ford Motor Company. Ford Motor Company allegedly produced a vehicle, the Pinto, that was considered a lethal hazard because of the placement of the gas tank. The tank was highly susceptible to puncture during a rear-end collision; it would experience considerable fuel leakage and produce fires when hit even at low speeds. There was evidence that Ford was fully aware of this problem in the initial stages of production but chose not to fix the Pinto's defect because it was not cost-efficient.

In light of the facts surrounding the accident, coupled with a revision in Indiana's criminal code, the Indiana State's Attorney decided to charge Ford with a criminal offense: reckless homicide. The State's Attorney convened a grand jury to consider an indictment under the reckless homicide statute. After entertaining testimony from both Ford officials and safety experts who had previously served as witnesses in civil cases against Ford, the grand jury unanimously returned indictments against Ford Motor Company for three counts of reckless homicide. Ford's handling of the Pinto situation subsequently came to symbolize what was wrong with corporate America.

The Trial

With the potential costs of a prosecution running high, Ford Motor Company attempted to see that the case would never come before a jury. The result of Ford's efforts was a motion that argued that the criminal indictment should be dismissed on both conceptual and constitutional grounds. Ford contended that the reckless homicide statute could not be applied to corporate entities. They also asserted that the use of the word "person" in other places in the criminal code clearly is not meant to apply to corporations. Conceptual consistency would thus preclude corporations from being charged with violent offenses such as reckless homicide. Ford's constitutional defense hinged on the fact that the National Traffic and Motor Vehicle Safety Act had already created a federal apparatus to supervise the automobile industry. The second, more serious, constitutional matter raised by Ford's lawyers involved the ex post facto provision of both the Indiana and United States Constitutions.

The prosecution was able to meet both the conceptual and constitutional defenses proposed by Ford. They argued that a person, as defined by Indiana code, was "a human being, corporation, partnership, unincorporated association, or governmental entity." Additionally, the prosecution noted that the Indiana criminal code explicitly read that a corporation may be prosecuted for an offense. There was no conceptual inconsistency in the code. With regard to the constitutional issues, the prosecution asserted that the federal agency was not intended to deprive states of their police power. Likewise, the ex post facto defense was faulty given Ford's interpretation of when its offense occurred. The prosecution maintained that the defendant's omissions in regard to its obligation to either repair the 1973 Pinto or warn the owners of the car's hazards were important elements of the offense.

The judge ruled that Ford could not be charged for recklessly designing and manufacturing the Pinto. Instead, Ford was allegedly reckless in repairing the vehicle. Ford could be charged with failure to repair. The case was now ready to go to trial.

The trial was moved to another locality because it was doubtful that Ford would receive an impartial hearing in the locality where the crash had occurred. Ford initially won some important rulings, including the restriction of the gruesome photos of the victims of the crash. The judge also agreed with Ford and barred nearly all materials that predated the manufacture year of the specific Pinto in question (1973). This meant that any safety tests conducted on the Pinto by Ford or the government would be suppressed.

The prosecution was limited to two major lines of argument. First, it called in auto safety experts, including a former Ford executive who testified that the fuel tank on the Pinto was placed in a potentially lethal position. Second, the prosecution relied upon eyewitnesses to prove that the Pinto exploded despite being hit at a relatively low speed. The Ford defense team had two witnesses who testified that one of the victims in the crash had stated that the car was stopped on the highway. If so, the speed at impact would have been more than 50 miles per hour, a collision that no small car could have withstood. The defense also reminded jurors that Ford had voluntarily agreed to recall the Pinto two months before this particular accident. Ford argued that they had done everything feasible to warn Pinto owners; it certainly had not been reckless in this duty.

After days of deliberation, the jurors returned their verdict: not guilty. While Ford's prosecution was not devoid of legal precedents, it was certainly the most poignant example of a corporation being brought within the reach of the criminal law for allegedly perpetrating violence against innocent citizens.

Chapter 19

The Corrections Corporation of America aka The Prison Realty Trust, Inc.

by Alan Mobley & Gilbert Geis

Key Concepts

"cherry picking"	inadequate training
conflict of interest	inmate abuse
excessive force	privatization

Introduction

The privatization of corrections was intended to reduce the deprivations and brutality of public correctional facilities, provide financial savings to taxpayers, and address the escalation of prison populations. Whether private organizations, such as Corrections Corporation of America, have met these expectation remains to be seen. This chapter serves as an initial critical assessment of privatization and specifically examines the problems that CCA has encountered during its operation.

The Evolution of CCA and The Prison Realty Trust

The Corrections Corporation of America (CCA) of Nashville, Tennessee, is the largest private prison enterprise in the United States. Thomas W. Beasley and Doctor R. Crants founded the CAA in 1983. CCA reportedly owns and operates 44 prisons and jails and manages 35 others and employs more than 14,000 individuals. During a five year period, from 1992 to 1997, CCA shares showed a compound annual growth rate of 70 percent. At one time, CCA was one of the five top performers on the New York Stock Exchange. In the late 1990s, the Corrections Corporation of America became CCA Prison Realty Trust (PRT) through a merger. CCA is now a real estate investment trust, or REIT, and pays no federal taxes. The Prison Realty Corporation also recently acquired another private correctional enterprise known as U.S. Corrections Corporation.

Lobbying for Leverage

CCA followed the example of managed health care or HMOs, in which service is driven by cost not need. Coincidentally, Massey Burch, which founded a major American HMO, also provided financial backing to Beasley's private correctional venture. As with an HMO, the CCA keeps costs down by controlling wages and benefits and purchasing in bulk. In addition to the connection with managed health care, the CCA has political ties was well. At one time, several prominent politicians in Tennessee, including the governor and speaker of the General Assembly, were stockholders in the CCA.

The Youngstown Debacle

CCA entered into a full-service detention contract with the District of Columbia. CCA purchased an abandoned industrial site from the city of Youngstown, Ohio, and constructed a $57 million prison. Youngstown, Ohio, is approximately 300 miles away from Washington, DC. Two fatal stabbings and 47 assaults occurred at the Youngstown prison within the first 14 months of operation. Shortly thereafter, six convicted murderers escaped from the facility. The separation of the prisoners from their families in the District of Columbia contributed to the trouble that exploded at the Youngstown prison. A large number of inmates had also been transferred into the prison, and the CCA staff was inexperienced. Furthermore, few educational and work opportunities were available to inmates. After the incident, the operating practices of CCA were called into question. In particular, CCA had misled local authorities in Youngstown and misclassified inmates in order to allow them into their Youngstown facility.

Jolts in Other Jurisdictions

CCA has endured a number of criticisms, including charges of inmate abuse in Tennessee and excessive force in Wisconsin. The Corporation has also been faulted for accepting only agreeable, able-bodied inmates and bidding on the best prison facilities in North Carolina. In some states, such as Florida, CCA forced inmates to pay for their own medical costs. CCA also came under fire in South Carolina for mistreating adolescent boys in a juvenile detention facility and in Texas for providing substandard living conditions.

Issues of Evaluation

Logan (1992) evaluated a CCA prison for women and compared it with one state-run facility. He found that the CCA compound outperformed the state prison. However, he did not examine recidivism. In fact, no one has examined the effectiveness of private corrections in terms of recidivism.

Staffing Private Prisons

Personnel costs are at the core of profitability; decreased labor costs actually increase profitability. CCA has attempted to reduce labor costs by employing fewer workers and paying them less than the state pays them. However, employing fewer workers may lead to a higher level of inmate containment and produce apathy, despair, and violence among the inmate population. Paying private correctional employees below the going state rate may also make them more prone to corruption. CCA most likely expects high turnover. CCA prisons are often managed by inexperienced crews.

Conclusion

The Corrections Corporation of America claimed that "a safe and secure correctional environment for staff, inmates and the community is paramount at ALL CCA facilities, all of which have numerous features designed to provide that secure environment" (Tatge, 1998c:4B). In light of the evidence presented in this chapter, it seems as if the company has seriously failed to realize the goals that it claimed to have set for itself.

Chapter 20

Ethics and Criminal Justice Research

by Belinda R. McCarthy & Robin J. King

Key Concepts

codes of ethics	randomization
coercing participation	self-determination
confidentiality	willingness to participate
privacy	

Problems Involving Work with Human Subjects

Stuart Cook (1976) lists the following ethical considerations surrounding research with human subjects:

1. Involving people in research without their knowledge.
2. Coercing people to participate.
3. Withholding from the participant the true nature of the research.
4. Deceiving the research participant.
5. Leading the research participant to commit acts that diminish their self-respect.
6. Violating the right to self-determination: research on behavior control and character change.
7. Exposing the research participant to physical or mental stress.
8. Invading the privacy of the research participant.
9. Withholding benefits from participants in control groups.
10. Failing to treat research participants fairly and to show them respect.

Balancing Scientific and Ethical Concerns

Cook (1976) identifies the potential benefits of a research project:

1. Advances in scientific theory that contribute to a general understanding of human behavior.
2. Advances in knowledge of practical value to society.
3. Gains for the research participant.

The potential cost to subjects are considerable, and it is often difficult for the researcher to be objective in assessing the issues. For this reason, many professional associations have established guidelines and procedures for ethical research conduct. The professional is honor-bound to follow these guide-lines.

Ethical/Political Considerations

Applied social research that examines the effectiveness of social policies and programs carries additional ethical responsibilities. Sometimes research results conflict with cherished beliefs. Researchers can expect findings such as these to meet with considerable resistance. Often the truth is very complicated. Researchers who are employed by an organization for which the research is being conducted face special problems because of the lack of freedom to pick and choose their topics. Also, researchers may be directly told to conceal or falsify results or they may be encouraged to design their research with an eye toward the desired results of the company or organization. Such research influences the course of human events in a real fashion—often work, education, future opportunities, and deeply held values and beliefs are affected by the outcomes.

The Purity of Scientific Research

The ideal of scientific inquiry is the pure, objective examination of the empirical world, untainted by personal prejudice. However, research is carried out by human beings who have a variety of motivations for undertaking the research they do. The availability of grants in a particular field may also encourage researchers to direct their attention to these areas. The need for university faculty to publish and establish a name for themselves in a particular area may encourage them to seek "hot" topics for their research or to identify an extremely narrow research focus in which they become identified as an expert. While none of these practices involves violations of ethical conduct, they should remind us that actions justified in the name of scientific inquiry may be motivated by factors far less "pure" than the objective they serve.

Chapter 21

Research Ethics and Research Funding:
A Case Study of Easy Virtue

by Gary W. Potter & Victor E. Kappeler

Key Concepts

> causal analysis vs. policy analysis
> conflict of interest
> false dichotomies
> federal funding trends
> pure research vs. applied research
> social construction of crime
> theory vs. practice

Introduction

As researchers and professors of scientific truth, criminologists carry a heavy social responsibility to be meticulously ethical in how they state that truth and how they conduct that research. Criminal justice research can impact the lives of many people. In particular, the sources of research funding may lead to major moral and ethical dilemmas in criminology and criminal justice research. Any researcher who has the expectation of financial support for research from a state agency, a salaried training relationship with an such an agency, or a consulting relationship with an agency has a moral responsibility to disclose those relationships at the outset and may have an ethical obligation to refrain from participating in evaluative research related to the agency. Criminologists should avoid conflicts of interest as well as the appearance of such conflicts.

The Social Construction of Crime by Funding Agencies

The availability of federal money for research has stimulated scientific inquiry concerning crime and justice, but also has dictated the topics to be studied, determined how they will be studied, and pointed to data sources for those studies. Federal funding agencies are altering the content, scope, and definitions of criminological research to fit their political agenda, not the objective criteria of social science. Federal funding agencies are serving as moral or political entrepreneurs in the social construction of a substantially incorrect reality of crime. For example, a review of NIJ research funds to universities reveals that the deviance of the poor as a subject of inquiry is emphasized while the deviance of the powerful is typically ignored. Furthermore, state definitions and ideologies of crime become embedded in scientific inquiry when scholars rely upon secondary data collected, processed, and stored by state agencies rather than their own collection of information.

Funding agencies also require particular types of data analysis and methodologies, thereby further controlling the growth of knowledge and direction of criminological inquiry. Quantitative analysis is favored by funding agencies because it allows policymakers to form sweeping generalizations. Qualitative research is more time-consuming, unbounded, and open-ended. Qualitative inquiry often points to the inconsistencies of social life, and such research may even lead to criticisms of official state agencies. Funding agencies do support qualitative work when such research achieves the desired outcomes, for example, by studying the best practices of the criminal justice system. The average (or worst) programs, practices, and agencies are never examined.

State Funding and Conflicts of Interest

It is often difficult for researchers in the criminal justice field to remain objective due to conflicts of interest that frequently emerge between the researcher and funding agency. When an institution offering research funding is itself a primary focus of the research, objectivity is difficult to maintain. In fact, many universities will hire a new faculty member on the basis of whether the applicant can fund his or her own position as opposed to whether the candidate can conduct scientific research or teach well. Furthermore, criminologists often have competing roles that they must play as researchers, practitioners, professors, and citizens living in their communities.

Theory vs. Practice

A fundamental false dichotomy in the research debate is that of theory versus practice. Without theory, there is no practice, there is no research, and there is no scholarship. Only through theory can criminologists structure, summarize, and develop reasonable explanations of reality based upon the available scientific evidence. Common sense, uninformed by theory, is neither very logical nor sensible. Theory should direct research and practice.

Causal Analysis vs. Policy Analysis

The false dichotomy between these two types of analysis (i.e., causal vs. policy) mirrors the problem of theory versus practice. Causal analysis is more theoretically informed; policy analysis is directed by practical or ideological notions. However, in reality, no problem is adequately addressed unless theory, which offers explanation of problems, is the grounding for policy.

Pure Research vs. Applied Research

Pure research is an end unto itself, and it is undertaken solely for the sake of its own merit and value. Applied research is a means to attain some end, usually a policy- or practice-related goal. This distinction is most likely false. The best research is both pure and applied. In a sense, the best research is based upon the scientific method. Such research is, first and foremost, objective. However, sound research must also be put in the proper context for understanding. Often, this requires scholars to present the whole truth as they presently know it and understand it, and not how they or their funding agency would like it to be.

Protecting Academic Freedom

Universities must protect academic freedom by rewarding pure research to a greater degree than applied or policy research. Universities must stop measuring productivity in dollars and start measuring it in effort. Universities must promote dialogue that raises fundamental dilemmas of science and fact. Universities must resist becoming the research arm of the state.

Chapter 22

Criminal Justice:
An Ethic for the Future

by Michael C. Braswell

Key Concepts

mindfulness
order-keeping
peacemaking

The Need for Mindfulness

If we are to develop an ethic for the future of criminal justice, we need to become more mindful and conscious of ethical truths concerning justice that are found in the present. We are all connected: parents to children, guards to prisoners, and offenders to victims. Although we are all bound together in society, we may still find it necessary to remove an offender from our midst. However, we must ensure that offenders are treated humanely on ethical and moral grounds. The promise of the future connects us in the knowledge that most offenders, especially with current overcrowding problems, will eventually return to our communities. Becoming more mindful can allow us, as individuals and communities, to take greater care in seeing and responding more meaningfully to the connections that bind us together in relationships.

Order-Keeping and Peacekeeping

Our search for justice can become subverted to a search for order only. We imagine that if we can just do things more efficiently, crime and justice problems can eventually be solved, or at least reduced to an insignificant level. However, this belief misses the larger truth. While keeping order is important, keeping peace is more than that.

Peacekeeping represents a larger vision for the individual and the community. If we are to contribute to a more just society, we must not simply think, talk, or write about peacekeeping and peacemaking, but personally struggle to be increasingly peaceful. Peacekeeping, in fact, becomes a practice of peacemaking.

Some Suggestions for Criminal Justice

If we are to look to the future of criminal justice with some measure of hope rather than a growing sense of cynicism, we must seek out fresh possibilities rather than defend traditional certainties. It seems more important than ever for us to look past our individual and agency interests into the larger community of which we are a part. Three areas in which this "wholesight" may be better employed within the criminal justice system are: (1) law and justice, (2) policing, and (3) corrections.

I. Law and Justice

The way we define laws and the way our justice system enforces them can enhance or diminish our opportunities for more peaceful and orderly communities. Additionally, issues of law and justice must be struggled with on a personal level. For example, it seems that many persons have come to believe that a legal act and a moral act are essentially the same. In life or in criminal court, when we do get caught, our plea is for mercy. Whether dealing with minor greed or major fraud, when we are the victim, we are inclined to want retribution, yet when we are the offender, we want mercy.

II. Policing

With more diversity within the ranks of policing, the opportunity exists for a greater openness in redefining police roles and functions. A clearer focus concerning the need for police officers to possess meaningful communication and interpersonal skills should become apparent. The more mindful police are with the ethic of care as translated through effective communication and interpersonal skills, the less likely they are to have to get tough with the people with whom they come in contact. Given the discretion and immediacy of response utilized by police officers in the community setting, there is perhaps no other criminal justice professional who is as connected to the community and who has as great an opportunity to contribute to the community's sense of care and well-being.

III. Corrections

Corrections directly addresses the "least of the community"—the "two-time losers," the nuisance factor, the disenfranchised, and the violent. We need to develop and more clearly articulate a treatment ethic that is restorative in nature and that more honestly addresses the community's sense of duty to itself. Because offenders are perceived as the least useful to the community, the larger community often feels, retributively, that such persons are deserving of the least care.

Justice as a Way Rather than a Destination

We need an ethic for the future that will empower us to act on an enlarged vision of what justice is about, a vision that will include the community of which we are all a part—the best of us and the worst of us—the best in *each* of us and the worst in *each* of us.

Justice as a way of service requires more than just the passionate zeal of the visionary, it also requires the mindfulness of quiet compassion. Only peace has the potential to remain calm and resolute even in the midst of suffering, which is an experience that connects each of us to the other in community. Peace comes from the inside out. People at peace with themselves create peaceful organizations that can then become instruments for peacemaking in the larger community.